Looking in the Forest

Written by Jonny Walker

Collins

Lots of living things feed and sleep near trees. Let's see if we can spot some!

If you look near the tree roots, you might see a bright slug.

This is a lemon slug. It roams near tree roots in forests. The lemon slug is bloated from chomping on mushrooms with its sharp teeth.

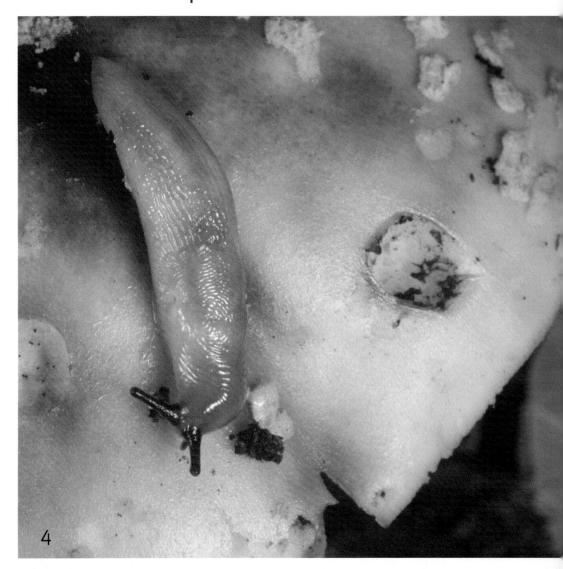

Now look for a stoat creeping by.
It has soft fur.

A stoat is a smart hunter. This one creeps up the tree's bark. It might raid a thrush's nest to get eggs.

This insect is a "forest bug". It has landed on a green fern frond.

Forest bugs slurp the sweet sap from oak trees. They munch insects too.

Can you see a toad? Toads sleep in mud or compost.

The toothless toad sucks up slugs. Toads can lurk unseen under twigs and sticks.

This is a treecreeper.
Its stiff tail helps it
clamber up tree trunks.

Treecreepers have long slender bills to help them hunt insects. This treecreeper has speared a moth.

When you next visit a forest, see what living things you can spot!

Looking in the forest

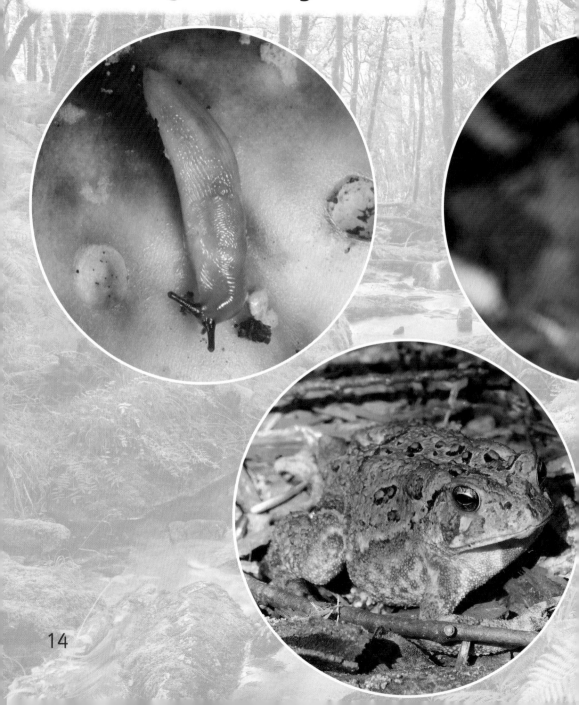

Review: After reading

Use your assessment from hearing the children read to choose any GPCs, words or tricky words that need additional practice.

Read 1: Decoding

- Let the children practise reading words with adjacent consonants, sounding out carefully to avoid missing any letters.

  b/l/oa/t/ed   th/r/u/sh/'s   c/l/a/m/b/er

  c/r/ee/p/i/ng   t/oo/th/l/e/ss   i/n/s/e/c/t/s

- Encourage the children to choose a page to read aloud, as fluently as possible. Say: Can you blend words in your head when you read your page?

Read 2: Prosody

- Model reading pages 8 and 9 to the children as if you are presenting a natural history documentary.

- Explain to the children that you have tried to use emphasis, pace and a questioning tone on page 9, to hold the listeners' interest.

- Ask the children to read pages 8 and 9. Say: Can you make the meaning clear and inspire the listeners with your enthusiasm?

Read 3: Comprehension

- Ask the children to describe any visits they've had to a wood or forest, or any TV programmes they have seen about a forest. What lived there? Were the living things easy to spot?

- Ask the children to look for words and phrases on the same page, to answer these questions.

  o page 6: What can the stoat do that shows it's a smart hunter? (*it "creeps up" so it can "raid a thrush's nest"*)

  o page 10: Which word shows that the toad is being careful not to be seen? (*lurk*)

  o page 12: What does the treecreeper use to spear a moth? (*long slender bill*)

- Look together at pages 14 and 15. Encourage the children to describe the animals in the pictures, using words from the book and their own ideas.